quick & easy healthy eating

quick & easy
healthy eating

Vincent Square Books

This edition published in 2004 by Vincent Square
Books, 3 Vincent Square, London SW1P 2LX

First published in 2003

ISBN 1 85626 596 X

Text © see page 176
Photographs © see page 176

The following are hereby identified as the authors of
this work in accordance with Section 77 of the
Copyright, Designs and Patents Act 1988: Darina
Allen, Hugo Arnold, Maddalena Bonino, Aliza
Baron Cohen, Ed Baines, Vatcharin Bhumichitr,
Conrad Gallagher, Paul Gayler, Elisabeth Luard,
Adrian Mercuri, Alison Price, Oded Schwartz,
Michael van Straten, Louisa J Walters and Mandy
Wagstaff.

A Cataloguing in Publication record for this title is
available from the British Library.

Printed and bound in China by C & C Offset
Printing Co., Ltd.

contents

introduction

How many of us want to improve our diets but think we just haven't got the time? This book will show you that it's perfectly possible to have a healthy diet without having to spend hours in the supermarket or the kitchen. All the recipes in this book take less than 45 minutes to prepare and cook, and most of them take less than half an hour. That's less time than it takes a takeaway to arrive, and is much better for you!

constructing a healthy diet

We are bombarded every day with messages about food. On the one hand, advertisements for convenience foods, fast food restaurants and confectionery. On the other, we hear about the latest health scare, or the latest superfoods. It can be difficult to see the wood for the trees, but the underlying principles of healthy eating haven't really changed for many years. Government guidelines suggest that a normal healthy diet consists of one third starchy foods, one third fruit and vegetables, with the other third made up of meat, fish or vegetarian alternatives, dairy products and sugars and fats. Most of us could do with cutting down on fats and sugars and increasing our intake of starchy wholegrain foods.

five a day

All of us should be aiming to eat at least 5 portions of fruit and vegetables per day. A portion counts as a slice of melon, an apple or half a grapefruit, 3 tablespoons of cooked vegetables such as peas, sweetcorn or carrots, or a cereal-bowl of salad. The health-giving benefits of increasing fruit and vegetable consumption are generally recognised. It is estimated that 5 portions of fruit and vegetables per day could reduce the risk of deaths from heart disease, stroke and cancer by up to 20 per cent in the population as a whole.

Sometimes it may seem difficult to incorporate 5 portions of fruit and vegetables in our diet, but it is not just fresh fruit and vegetables that are important. A glass of pure fruit juice counts as a portion, as does a tablespoon of raisins, or 3 dried apricots. Frozen vegetables are as good, if not better, than some fresh vegetables as many of them are frozen immediately after picking – conserving valuable nutrients that can be depleted after a lengthy stay in a warehouse, or on the supermarket shelves.

All fruit and vegetables contain Vitamins A, C and E, but some are richer sources than others. As a general rule, the darker or brighter the colour of the vegetable the better – dark green, deep red, purple, yellow and bright orange fruit and vegetables normally have the highest levels of vitamins and minerals. Broccoli, carrots, spinach, oranges and peppers are just a few of the most vitamin-packed fruits and vegetables. Concentrate on adding colour to your shopping basket and you will automatically increase your consumption of vital nutrients.

Variety is also important. Research is still being done on the way combinations of food react in the body to provide us with their nutrients but we do know that eating a wide variety of foods, especially fruit and vegetables, increases our chances of consuming all the vitamins and minerals we need. And the more variety we eat the more we are likely to enjoy our food rather than getting bored with eating the same thing day after day.

tips & shortcuts

healthy cooking

One of the simplest ways of reducing the fat content of your food is simply to measure it. Instead of glugging a pool of oil into the frying pan, measure out a tablespoon and pour that in. Use a non-stick frying pan and you will not need any oil at all for some fried foods. You may be surprised at how a little oil can go a long way. In the same way you can cut down on salad dressing by measuring a tablespoonful and pouring it over your salad. Use the salad dressing to coat the salad rather than to drown it. Another good way to enjoy the taste of fried food while cutting down on the fat is to use a ridged grill pan. Heat the pan and use a cook's brush to brush the food with a small amount of oil. When the pan is hot, place the food on the grill and cook on both sides. Any fat that comes off the meat will drain away into the ridges of the pan.

box schemes

If there is an organic vegetable box service operating in your area, you might consider joining it. This will cut down on shopping time but will also present you with a range of unusual vegetables which you may not often buy. Variety is important in the consumption of fruit and vegetables, so it can force you to be creative in order to use up all your vegetables before the next box of surprises arrives.

use your freezer

Take advantage of the wide range of frozen produce available but don't buy lots of frozen ready-meals; stock up instead on frozen vegetables which you can whip out and add to any meal. There's a lot more out there these days than just frozen peas. Add mixed frozen vegetables to a Spanish omelette or add green beans and sweetcorn to a plain frozen pizza, or just use them as easy accompaniment to any meal.

how to use this book

Each recipe provides information about the number of servings it provides, and how long it takes to prepare and cook. As a general principle, the preparation time is the time it takes to wash, prepare and chop the ingredients for the recipe, and the cooking time is the time you actually need to spend cooking, although for much of this time the dish may be able to be left to its own devices while you get on with something else.

In addition, each recipe provides nutritional information. As a rough guide, children, sedentary women and older adults need approximately 1,600 calories per day. Teenage girls, active women and sedentary men need 2,200 calories, and teenage boys, active men and very active women need up to 2,800 per day. Current advice is that no more than 10-30 per cent of our daily energy intake should come from fats. Most of us should be trying to cut down on total fats, and particularly saturated fats.

Carbohydrates are an important part of everyone's diet. It is recommended that at least a third of our daily intake is made up of starchy foods such as potatoes, yams, wholegrain bread, pasta, noodles, chapattis, rice, sweet potatoes and so on.

It is recommended that our daily salt intake not exceed 6g. Most of us consume more like 9g (the equivalent of 2 teaspoonfuls). Much of the salt we consume comes from processed convenience foods, but approximately 10 per cent of it comes from salt we add to our food, either during cooking or at the table. High salt consumption is implicated in raised blood pressure, which in turn has been linked to a higher risk of heart disease and stroke. There is evidence that the fibre contained in wholegrain foods and in fruit and vegetables may protect against developing some forms of heart disease and cancer.

better
breakfasts

orange & pineapple smoothie

100ml (3$\frac{1}{2}$fl oz) freshly squeezed orange juice

100ml (3$\frac{1}{2}$fl oz) pineapple juice

2 dessertspoons honey

8 ice cubes

juice of $\frac{1}{2}$ lemon

Place all ingredients in a liquidiser, blend well and serve immediately.

TIP

This smoothie is particularly high in Vitamin C.

Nutritional value per serving:

Calories: 125

Fats: 0g

Carbohydrates: 32g

Salt: 0.03g

Saturated fat: 0g

Fibre: 0.1g

strawberry & raspberry smoothie

10 raspberries

6 strawberries

1 banana

juice of 1 orange

10 ice cubes

Blend well in a liquidiser and serve immediately.

TIP

This smoothie is particularly high in Vitamin C.

Nutritional value per serving:

Calories: 144

Fats: 0g

Carbohydrates: 34g

Salt: 0.02g

Saturated fat: 0.1g

Fibre: 3g

fruit-filled melon shells

175g (6oz) of mixed strawberries, blueberries,
blackberries and redcurrants

1 ripe cantaloupe melon, halved and deseeded

Wash the berries carefully, removing any hulls.

Wash the currants and strip them from their stalks, but don't bother to hull them – you'll still be there at lunchtime.

Heap the soft fruit into the hollows in the melon and serve.

TIP

This breakfast is high in Vitamins A and C.

Nutritional value per serving:

Calories: 68

Fats: 0g

Carbohydrates: 14g

Salt: 0.08g

Saturated fat: 0g

Fibre: 4.2g

compote of dried fruit

350g (12oz) mixed dried fruits – prunes,
  apricots, mangos, raisins, blueberries, apples,
  bananas or any other that take your fancy
300g (10oz) natural bio-yogurt, preferably
  organic
2 tablespoons flax seeds

Put the fruit in a large bowl and cover with boiling water. Allow to cool, then put into the fridge overnight.

In the morning, drain the fruit. Arrange the fruit and yogurt on two plates and sprinkle the flax seeds on top.

TIP

This breakfast is particularly high in iron, calcium and fibre.

Nutritional value per serving:
Calories: 533
Fats: 9g
Carbohydrates: 105g
Salt: 0.52g
Saturated fat: 3.5g
Fibre: 12.1g

honey, fruit & yogurt

2 bananas, peeled and sliced

150g (5oz) raspberries

300g (10oz) natural organic bio-yogurt

2 tablespoons honey, preferably organic

Divide the banana slices between 2 bowls.

Gently wash the raspberries, taking care not to bruise them, and pile on top of the bananas.

Tip half the yogurt on top of each bowl.

Drizzle with the honey.

TIP

This breakfast is particularly high in calcium and Vitamin C.

Nutritional value per serving:

Calories: 271

Fats: 6g

Carbohydrates: 48g

Salt: 0.39g

Saturated fat: 2.9g

Fibre: 3g

oatmeal porridge

160g (5^1/$_2$oz) oatmeal
1 litre (1^3/$_4$ pints) water
1 level teaspoon salt
single cream or milk, to serve
soft brown sugar, to serve

Bring the water to the boil and sprinkle in the oatmeal gradually, stirring all the time. Put over a low heat and stir until the water comes back to the boil. Cover and simmer for 15-20 minutes, stirring occasionally.

Add the salt and stir again. Serve with single cream or milk and soft brown sugar melting over the top.

TIP
Leftover porridge can be stored in a covered container in the fridge – it will reheat perfectly the next day.

Nutritional value per serving:
Calories: 160
Fats: 3g
Carbohydrates: 29g
Salt: 1.3g
Saturated fat: 0.7g
Fibre: 2.7g

muesli

4 tablespoons rolled oats

3 tablespoons water

2 large dessert apples e.g. Cox's Orange Pippin

1 teaspoon honey

Measure out the water into a bowl and sprinkle the oatmeal on top. Let the oatmeal soak up the water while you grate the apples, using the largest side to grate the apple coarsely, skin and all. Pick out the pips.

Stir the honey into the oatmeal and then stir in the grated apple. Taste; if it needs a little more honey add it; this depends on how much you heaped up on the spoon earlier on.

Divide it between 2 bowls. Have one yourself and give the other to your favourite person that morning. It tastes delicious just like that but will taste even scrummier if you sprinkle over a little soft brown Barbados sugar and a little runny cream.

TIP

Muesli is a good source of fibre.

Nutritional value per serving:

Calories: 140

Fats: 2g

Carbohydrates: 29g

Salt: 0.01g

Saturated fat: 0.3g

Fibre: 4.6g

lig
lunch

tomato, **mozzarella** & avocado salad

175g (6oz) mixed dried fruits – dates, stoneless
  prunes, apricots, raisins, etc. – cut into
  raisin-sized pieces
1 quantity standard French dressing (see below)
350g (12oz) fresh, young mozzarella cheese,
  drained and sliced
4 large tomatoes, sliced
2 kiwi fruit, peeled and sliced
2 avocados, peeled, stoned and sliced
  lengthways

Soak all the fruits in freshly boiled water for 5 minutes. Drain thoroughly and stir into the dressing.

Arrange the slices of tomato, mozzarella, kiwi fruit and avocado, in that order, on 4 plates.

Pour the French dressing over the top.

TIP

A good source of calcium, Vitamins A, B6, C and E, as well as fibre.

To make enough French dressing to dress a salad for 4 people, place 6 tablespoons of extra-virgin olive oil, 2 tablespoons of white wine vinegar, salt and freshly ground pepper in a screw-top jar and shake to combine thoroughly. Dress the salad just before serving.

Nutritional value per serving:
Calories: 655
Fats: 49g
Carbohydrates: 30g
Salt: 1.67g
Saturated fat: 15.9g
Fibre: 5.4g

pickled herring with potato & tomato salad

350g (12oz) new potatoes, such as Charlotte

4 rollmop herrings

110g (4oz) semi sun-dried tomatoes, cubed

4 tablespoons extra-virgin olive oil

Scrub the potatoes, but don't peel them. Place in a saucepan of water, bring to the boil and cook until just tender. Leave to cool slightly.

Unwrap the rollmops, keeping all the onion inside, and place each one on a plate.

Quarter the potatoes and mix with the tomatoes. Drizzle with the olive oil.

Serve the potato and tomato mixture alongside the herrings.

Nutritional value per serving:

Calories: 378

Fats: 21g

Carbohydrates: 29g

Salt: 2.62g

Saturated fat: 3.2g

Fibre: 0.9g

prawn, potato & basil salad

450g (1lb) new potatoes, diced
2 tablespoons basil leaves, torn into pieces
50g(2oz) radishes, sliced
1 spring onion, chopped
juice of ½ lime
150g (5oz) plain yogurt
225g (8oz) peeled prawns
salt and freshly ground black pepper
a few lettuce leaves, to serve

Boil the potatoes until tender, drain and leave to cool. Place in a bowl with the basil, radishes, spring onion, lime juice and yogurt and mix well. Season to taste. Just before serving, gently mix in the prawns. Arrange a few lettuce leaves on each plate and place the prawn salad on top. Serve immediately.

TIP
This salad is rich in calcium, and Vitamins B6 and C.

Nutritional value per serving:
Calories: 316
Fats: 3g
Carbohydrates: 42g
Salt: 5.26g
Saturated fat: 0.7g
Fibre: 2.5g

cypriot salad

50g (2oz) haloumi cheese, cut into 5mm (¼in)
  slices

4 medium tomatoes

¼ cucumber, sliced

¼ yellow pepper, cored, deseeded and diced

1 handful of flat-leaf parsley, roughly chopped

10 black olives, stoned

½ red onion, thinly sliced

3-4 large lettuce leaves, torn into pieces

Dressing

2 tablespoons extra-virgin olive oil

1 tablespoon white wine vinegar

1-2 teaspoons lemon juice

sea salt and freshly ground black pepper

Toast the cheese under a medium grill on a non-stick baking sheet until golden brown. Turn once and brown the other side. Mix with the other ingredients in a large salad bowl. Shake all the dressing ingredients together in a glass jar until well combined. Pour over the salad, gently toss to mix and serve immediately.

TIP

Haloumi is available in many Mediterranean delicatessens. If you can't get hold of it, you can substitute feta.

This salad is high in Vitamins A, C and E.

Nutritional value per serving:

Calories: 251

Fats: 20g

Carbohydrates: 11g

Salt: 2.33g

Saturated fat: 5.6g

Fibre: 3.8g

beetroot, rocket, apple & cashew nut salad

1 large or 2 small fresh beetroot, peeled
   and grated
1 dessert apple, grated
25-50g (1-2oz) fresh rocket, washed
   and chopped
25g (1oz) cashew nuts, chopped
1 carrot, peeled

Dressing
1 dessertspoon extra-virgin olive oil
3 dessertspoons fresh lemon juice
sea salt and freshly ground black pepper

Place the beetroot, apple and rocket in a salad bowl.

Place the cashew nuts on a baking sheet under the grill on medium heat, and toast until golden brown. Turn once or twice to brown all sides. With a vegetable peeler, cut thick shavings off the peeled carrot. Add the shavings to the bowl with the cashew nuts and mix well.

Make the dressing by shaking all the ingredients together in a glass jar until well mixed. Pour over the salad and toss gently to coat. Serve immediately.

TIP

This salad is rich in folic acid and Vitamins A and C.

Nutritional value per serving:
Calories: 176
Fats: 11g
Carbohydrates: 17g
Salt: 0.61g
Saturated fat: 1.31g
Fibre: 3.5g

salad with tuna-stuffed bell pepper

2 large yellow peppers

185g (6½oz) can of tuna in olive oil, drained

1 tablespoon rinsed, chopped capers

3-4 tablespoons mayonnaise (preferably home-made)

200g (7oz) bag of mixed salad leaves

6 tablespoons French dressing (see page 30)

Preheat the oven to 180°C/350°F/gas mark 4. Arrange the peppers on a baking sheet. Roast for 8-10 minutes until the skins are slightly blistered and the peppers are tender, but still holding their shape.

Transfer the peppers to a large bowl, cover with cling film and leave to cool completely - this will help steam the skins off. Carefully peel away the skins, then cut each pepper in half and remove the stalks and inner membrane.

Finely chop the tuna, then transfer to a bowl and add the capers and season to taste. Mix in enough of the mayonnaise to bind and then fill the pepper halves - this will also help them to keep their shape.

Place the salad leaves in a bowl, season and pour in half of the dressing, tossing to coat. Arrange on serving plates and place a stuffed pepper on top of each one. Drizzle the remaining dressing over the stuffed pepper halves and serve immediately.

TIP

A good source of Vitamins B6, C and E.

Nutritional value per serving:

Calories: 338

Fats: 30g

Carbohydrates: 6g

Salt: 1.15g

Saturated fat: 4.4g

Fibre: 2.1g

stir-fried vegetables with prawns

1 tablespoon light soy sauce

1 tablespoon sherry vinegar

$^1/_2$ teaspoon Tabasco sauce

1 tablespoon sesame oil

1 teaspoon runny honey

2 tablespoons rapeseed oil – preferably organic, but certainly GM-free

2 carrots, finely sliced

110g (4oz) oyster mushrooms, sliced

1 head broccoli, cut into uniform-sized florets

2 heads pak choi, cut into 8 lengthways

1.5cm ($^1/_2$in) fresh ginger root, peeled and grated

5 fat spring onions, quartered lengthways

175g (6oz) mangetout, cut into 2cm ($^3/_4$in) pieces

8 raw king tiger prawns in their shells

450g (1lb) fresh beansprouts

4 tablespoons sesame seeds

Whisk together the soy sauce, sherry vinegar, Tabasco sauce, sesame oil, and runny honey and set aside.

Heat the rapeseed oil in a wok or large, deep-sided frying pan. Add the carrots, mushrooms, broccoli, pak choi and ginger and stir-fry, stirring continuously, for 3 minutes. Add the spring onions and mangetout and continue cooking for 1 minute.

Tip in the prawns and cook for 4 minutes, until they start to change colour. Tip in the beansprouts and cook for 1 minute. Add the soy sauce mixture and 3 tablespoons water and cook gently until the vegetables are tender – about 4 minutes.

Meanwhile, dry-fry the sesame seeds in a separate pan.

Serve the stir-fry with the sesame seeds scattered on top.

TIP

This dish is packed full of goodness - as well as iron, fibre, calcium and folic acid, it also has good doses of Vitamins A, B6, C and E.

Nutritional value per serving:

Calories: 307

Fats: 19g

Carbohydrates: 14g

Salt: 1.23g

Saturated fat: 2.1g

Fibre: 7g

cornish crab & asparagus salad

12 asparagus spears, peeled and well trimmed

2 heads of chicory

2 avocados, peeled, stoned and sliced

2 carrots, cut into matchsticks

310g (11oz) fresh white crabmeat

salt and freshly ground black pepper

Parmesan shavings, to garnish

Lemon, mustard & Parmesan vinaigrette

1 tablespoon Dijon mustard

1 small egg yolk

1 tablespoon lemon juice

finely grated zest of $1/2$ lemon

1 tablespoon Champagne vinegar or white
 wine vinegar

5 tablespoons extra-virgin olive oil

$1^1/_2$ tablespoons freshly grated Parmesan

Cook the asparagus spears in boiling salted water for 3-4 minutes or until just tender. Drain and refresh in cold water, then dry them thoroughly and cut lengthways in half.

For the dressing, whisk together the mustard, egg yolk, lemon juice and zest and vinegar, then whisk in the olive oil. Add the grated Parmesan cheese and season to taste.

Pull the leaves from the chicory, wash and dry them and arrange in a salad bowl or on serving plates. Put the asparagus, avocado, carrots and crabmeat in a separate bowl and toss gently with the dressing, then adjust the seasoning. Scatter this mixture over the chicory leaves, sprinkle some coarsely cracked black pepper over the top and then scatter with the Parmesan shavings. Serve immediately.

TIP

Vegetarians can easily omit the crabmeat and replace it with more vegetables. Globe artichoke hearts, for example, would go rather well.

TIP

A nutrient-rich salad containing zinc, folic acid, fibre as well as Vitamins A, B6, C and E.

Nutritional value per serving:

Calories: 452

Fats: 37g

Carbohydrates: 8g

Salt: 1.59g

Saturated fat: 6g

Fibre: 5.2g

spiced indian crab

1 tablespoon unscented vegetable oil

1 medium onion, finely chopped

2 garlic cloves, finely chopped

3 teaspoon medium-hot curry powder

$1/2$ teaspoon brown mustard seeds

1 teaspoon ground cumin

$1/2$ teaspoon chilli powder

2 tablespoons chicken stock

450g (1lb) picked white crabmeat, shelled

$1/4$ teacup washed and dried coriander leaves

juice of 2 lemons

salt and freshly ground black pepper

To garnish

4 tablespoons yogurt

30 coriander leaves, picked, washed and dried

Heat the oil in a saucepan, add the onion and garlic and cook until soft, without browning. Add the spices and cook for a further 2-3 minutes, then pour in the stock and cook on a low heat for 10 minutes.

In a bowl mix the crabmeat, coriander and lemon juice into the spice mixture. Season with salt and pepper.

To serve on spoons, lay teaspoons on a tray. Use a spare teaspoon to mould the crab paste on to each teaspoon. To serve, top each with a little yogurt and a coriander leaf.

TIP

You can serve this on spoons as a canapé or use it as an excellent sandwich filling or topping for a baked potato.

This dish contains good quantities of iron and zinc.

Nutritional value per serving:

Calories: 212

Fats: 10g

Carbohydrates: 6g

Salt: 1.57g

Saturated fat: 1.3g

Fibre: 1.4g

lobster & mango salad

selection of salad leaves e.g. lollo rosso,
  butterhead, iceberg, oakleaf, rocket,
  watercress
1 ripe mango
350g (12oz) lobster tail and claw meat – a
  900g-1.1kg (2-2$\frac{1}{2}$lb) lobster should yield
  this quantity
sprigs of fennel, chervil and borage flowers, to
  garnish

Dressing
6 tablespoons extra-virgin olive oil
2 tablespoons lemon juice, freshly squeezed
salt and freshly ground pepper
pinch of sugar
2 teaspoons parsley, freshly chopped

Wash and dry the salad leaves. Combine all the ingredients for the dressing. Peel the mango and cut into slices or dice depending on presentation; sprinkle with lemon juice.

To assemble: toss the salad leaves in just enough dressing to make the leaves glisten. Arrange a little mound on each plate.

Nutritional value per serving:
Calories: 201
Fats: 12g
Carbohydrates: 10g
Salt: 0.66g
Saturated fat: 1.7g
Fibre: 1.9g

tropical **salad**

small bunch of coriander

1 mango

1 papaya

400g (14oz) tin of palm hearts, drained

200g (7oz) small peeled prawns, plus 12 large
   peeled prawns, to garnish

a small bunch of spring onions, thinly sliced

lime halves, to garnish

Dressing

grated zest and juice of 1 lime

1 tablespoon soy sauce

$1/2$ fresh red chilli, deseeded and finely chopped

1 garlic clove, finely chopped

1 teaspoon freshly grated ginger

3 tablespoons vegetable oil

pulp from 1 passion fruit

$1/2$ teaspoon sugar

Remove the stalks from the coriander, discard any woody sections and chop the stalks finely for the dressing.

Make the dressing: in a bowl, mix all the ingredients with the finely chopped coriander stalks. Chill in the fridge while you prepare the salad.

To make the salad: first peel the mango and cut it into slices around the central stone. Cut the papaya into quarters, scoop out the seeds, then cut the papaya away from the skin, as you would a melon. Add the pieces of fruit to a bowl. Cut the palm hearts into bite-sized pieces and add them to the fruit. Add the small prawns to the bowl, then stir in the coriander leaves and spring onion. Pour over the dressing and toss the salad.

Pour into a serving dish, scatter the large prawns over the top and garnish with the lime halves.

TIP

This salad contains fibre, along with Vitamins A and C.

Nutritional value per serving:

Calories: 297

Fats: 10g

Carbohydrates: 25g

Salt: 5.26g

Saturated fat: 1.2g

Fibre: 5.5g

spicy prawn couscous

175g (6oz) raisins

350g (12oz) couscous

450ml (16fl oz) vegetable stock

225g (8oz) cooked, peeled shrimp

1/2 large cucumber, peeled, deseeded and cubed

1 red pepper, deseeded and cubed

1 green pepper, deseeded and cubed

4 large plum tomatoes, deseeded and roughly
  chopped

4 spring onions, finely chopped

1 large carrot, grated

1 fine-skinned courgette, grated

Dressing

125ml (4fl oz) olive oil

125ml (4fl oz) walnut oil

2 small red chillies, deseeded and finely
  chopped

3 large spring onions, trimmed and finely sliced

1 garlic clove, chopped

2.5cm (1in) fresh ginger, peeled and grated

Mix all the ingredients for the dressing together in a screw-top jar and shake to combine.

Put the raisins into freshly boiled water for 1 minute. Drain.

Add the raisins to the couscous and cook according to packet instructions – this usually takes about 20 minutes – using stock instead of water.

Add the prawns and raw vegetables while the couscous is still hot. Pour on the dressing and stir to mix.

Serve while still warm, or cover with cling film and leave in the fridge. Bring back to room temperature before serving.

TIP

This lunch provides good amounts of iron, calcium and Vitamins A, B6, C and E.

Nutritional value per serving:

Calories: 480

Fats: 30g

Carbohydrates: 40g

Salt: 3g

Saturated fat: 3.5g

Fibre: 2.5g

spicy noodles with tomatoes

110g (4oz) egg noodles, cooked

3 tablespoons sunflower oil

$1/2$ teaspoon cumin seeds

5 garlic cloves, finely chopped

1 green chilli, finely chopped

1 teaspoon freshly grated ginger

good pinch ground asafetida, optional

$1/4$ teaspoon ground turmeric

$1/4$-$1/2$ teaspoon cayenne pepper

6 ripe tomatoes, peeled and coarsely chopped

110g (4oz) onion, finely chopped

salt, freshly ground pepper and sugar

3 tablespoons fresh coriander leaves,
   finely chopped

Cook the noodles according to the instructions on the packet. Drain and reserve.

Heat the oil in a wok or large, preferably non-stick frying pan over a medium-high heat.

When hot, add the cumin seeds, stir for a few seconds. Add the garlic, chilli and ginger. Stir and fry for 2-3 minutes until the garlic begins to colour. Add the asafetida, if using, turmeric and cayenne pepper. Stir very quickly and then, add the onions and cook for 3 or 4 minutes on a medium heat. Then toss in the chopped tomatoes, season with salt, pepper and sugar and cook for 5-6 minutes stirring frequently. Add the coriander, taste and correct seasoning.

Simmer for 2-3 minutes or until the tomatoes are tender. Stir the noodles into the tomato mixture. Bubble for a minute or two to heat the noodles through. Serve immediately with lots of fresh coriander.

TIP

There's plenty of Vitamins C and E in this dish.

Nutritional value per serving:

Calories: 228

Fats: 11g

Carbohydrates: 28g

Salt: 0.41g

Saturated fat: 1.3g

Fibre: 1.9g

green & red pasta salad

400g (14oz) mixed tomato and spinach fusilli
   pasta
florets of 1 large head broccoli, very large ones
   halved
150g (5oz) baby spinach
1 red onion, very finely chopped
200g (7oz) seedless black grapes, halved
125ml (4fl oz) extra-virgin olive oil
3 tablespoons freshly grated Parmesan cheese

Cook the pasta according to the packet instructions. Drain and put into a large, warm bowl. Meanwhile, plunge the broccoli into a saucepan of fast boiling water for 5 minutes. Wash the spinach, leaving any water still clinging to the leaves. Place in another pan, cover and cook until wilted – this should take 3-5 minutes, depending on the age of the leaves.

Drain the green vegetables and tip them into the pasta with the onion and grapes. Stir gently but thoroughly, being careful not to break up the broccoli florets. Pour the olive oil over the mixture, add the Parmesan, mix gently again and serve.

How to dice an onion

Cut the onion in half from top to bottom. Peel the skin, leaving the root intact. With half an onion cut-side down, make horizontal cuts towards the root, then cut the onion lengthways. Finally cut the onion crossways into dice.

Nutritional value per serving:

Calories: 730

Fats: 34g

Carbohydrates: 89g

Salt: 0.4g

Saturated fat: 5.9g

Fibre: 7.6g

egg noodles with stir-fried vegetables

110g (4oz) noodles, dried or fresh

2 tablespoons vegetable oil

1 garlic clove, finely chopped

1 large dried red chilli, roughly chopped

50g (2oz) celery, finely chopped

50g (2oz) beansprouts

2 spring onions, finely chopped

1 medium tomato, cut into segments

$1/2$ teaspoon chilli powder

3 tablespoons light soy sauce

1 teaspoon dark soy sauce

$1/2$ teaspoon granulated sugar

Bring a pan of water to the boil for the noodles. If using fresh noodles, shake the strands loose, place in a sieve or strainer and lower into the boiling water for 2-3 seconds, or until heated through. If using dried noodles, cook in the boiling water until the strands separate, by which time they will be soft. Drain and set aside.

In a wok, heat the oil until a light haze appears. Add the garlic and fry for 2-3 seconds, then add the chilli and continue to stir-fry until the garlic is golden brown.

Add the cooked noodles to the pan, stir well to prevent them from sticking, then add all the remaining ingredients, stirring quickly. Turn on to a serving dish and serve.

Nutritional value per serving:

Calories: 170

Fats: 7g

Carbohydrates: 23g

Salt: 2.31g

Saturated fat: 1g

Fibre: 1.4g

chicken with peppers, guacamole & chilli oil

4 chicken breasts, skinned and each cut
    into 5 strips
chilli oil
2 cos lettuces, large leaves torn in half
1 can Spanish red peppers, drained and halved
1 bunch coriander

Guacamole
3 ripe avocados, peeled and stoned
juice of $\frac{1}{2}$ lemon
1 clove garlic, crushed
1 medium chilli, deseeded and diced
$\frac{1}{2}$ medium red onion, diced
$\frac{1}{2}$ bunch of coriander, roughly chopped
salt and freshly ground black pepper

To make the guacamole, mash the avocado with a fork or in a food processor. Mix in the lemon juice, garlic, chilli, onion and chopped coriander. Season to taste.

Preheat the chargrill or griddle pan and lightly brush the chicken with some chilli oil. Place the chicken strips on the pan and grill for 5 minutes on both sides until the chicken is golden brown.

To serve, spoon some guacamole onto each plate. Top with cos lettuce and arrange some chicken and peppers on top. Spoon some more guacamole onto each plate and drizzle with chilli oil. Serve immediately.

How to pangrill chicken breasts

Heat a ridged grill pan. Brush each chicken breast (not the grill) with a little sesame oil, then season the chicken breasts and place on the grill. Cook for 5-6 minutes on each side, until lightly charred and cooked through.

Nutritional value per serving:
Calories: 402
Fats: 24g
Carbohydrates: 10g
Salt: 0.61g
Saturated fat: 3.1g
Fibre: 5.8g

delicious
dinners

steamed citrus **mussels**

1 garlic clove, crushed

1cm ($\frac{1}{2}$in) root ginger, peeled and finely sliced

2 stems fresh lemongrass, outer leaves removed
and finely chopped

50ml (2fl oz) rice wine vinegar or white
wine vinegar

50ml (2fl oz) dry white wine (optional) or water

juice of $\frac{1}{2}$ lemon

1.2kg (2lb) fresh mussels, beards removed and
well scrubbed

75ml (3fl oz) reduced-fat coconut milk

juice of 1 lime

Place the garlic, ginger, lemongrass, vinegar, wine and lemon juice in a large pan, bring to the boil and simmer for 5 minutes. Add the mussels to the pan, cover with a lid and cook over a low heat for 3-4 minutes, shaking the pan occasionally. When the mussels open, add the coconut milk and the lime juice, cover and shake once or twice to coat all the mussels in the sauce. Discard any mussels which are not open and serve immediately.

TIP

There are high levels of iron and zinc in this dish.

How to debeard mussels

To remove the beards from mussels, hold the mussel with the pointed end away from you. Pull downwards on the beard to remove it. Scrub the mussels well before cooking.

Nutritional value per serving:

Calories: 181

Fats: 7g

Carbohydrates: 7g

Salt: 1.45g

Saturated fat: 3.8g

Fibre: 0.2g

scallops with ginger, spring onion & tamarind

1 tablespoon tamarind paste

2cm ($^3/_4$in) piece of ginger, peeled and grated

2 spring onions, thinly sliced lengthways and
 soaked in iced water

3 tablespoons vegetable oil, plus more for
 the pan

1 tablespoon toasted sesame oil

12 scallops

salt

Place the tamarind paste in a saucepan with 4 tablespoons of water and heat gently, stirring to extract as much of the tamarind as possible. Set aside and allow to cool.

Strain and combine with the grated ginger, drained spring onions and both types of oil.

Season the scallops with salt. Get a frying pan good and hot and then oil it lightly. When the oil is hot, fry the scallops over as high a heat as you can manage for no more than 45 seconds on each side.

Place the scallops on small shallow plates or, better still, in well-scrubbed scallop shells, and spoon over the tamarind mixture.

TIP

If the scallops are really thick, they will sometimes remain cold and uncooked in the middle in the time it takes the exterior to cook perfectly. You can avoid this – and make the scallops go further – by cutting them across into two rounds.

Nutritional value per serving:

Calories: 263

Fats: 18g

Carbohydrates: 3g

Salt: 0.92g

Saturated fat: 2.3g

Fibre: 0.1g

seared scallops with guacamole, coriander & chilli

1 avocado

juice of 1 lemon

juice of 1 lime

50g (2oz) coriander leaves, chopped

1 clove garlic, chopped

1 chilli, deseeded and diced

50g (2oz) chives, chopped

1 tablespoon olive oil

25g (1oz) butter

12 fresh scallops

2 tablespoons reduced-fat coconut milk

coriander sprigs

salt and freshly ground black pepper

Avocado salad

1 avocado, diced

1 chilli, deseeded and diced

40g (1¹/₂oz) coriander leaves, chopped

Peel and stone the avocado and dice finely. Place in a small bowl, add the lemon and lime juice and season with salt and pepper. Process the coriander, garlic, chilli and chives in a food processor, then mix in with the avocado.

Heat the olive oil and butter in a small frying pan. Season the scallops then sear for 1 minute on each side. Mix the ingredients for the salad in a bowl. Serve the scallops with spoonfuls of guacamole and avocado salad.

Garnish with coconut milk and coriander.

How to prepare scallops

With the flat side of the scallop upwards, slide a sharp knife between the two halves of the shell to cut the nerve holding them closed. Remove and discard the top shell. Slide the knife underneath the exposed scallop and ease it off the shell. Discard the black tissue around it and cut off the black vein that runs around the side of the scallop.

Nutritional value per serving:

Calories: 345

Fats: 26g

Carbohydrates: 3g

Salt: 1.14g

Saturated fat: 7.9g

Fibre: 2.7g

clams with chilli & basil

450g (1lb) fresh baby clams in their shells
2 tablespoons vegetable oil
2 garlic cloves, finely chopped
1 tablespoon chilli oil
2 tablespoons *nam pla* (Thai fish sauce)
2 tablespoons fish stock or water
$^1/_2$ teaspoon granulated sugar
1 long fresh red chilli, finely slivered
20 fresh holy basil leaves, shredded

Rinse the clams under cold water, discarding any that do not close when shaken. Drain and set aside.

In a wok or frying pan, heat the oil and fry the garlic until golden brown. Add the clams and chilli oil and stir thoroughly. Add all the remaining ingredients in turn, stirring after each addition, and cook over a high heat until the clams open. Discard any clams that remain closed.

Pour into a serving bowl and serve.

TIP

If you can't find holy basil, use ordinary basil instead.

Nutritional value per serving:
Calories: 1.5
Fats: 9g
Carbohydrates: 2g
Salt: 1.43g
Saturated fat: 1.1g
Fibre: 0.1g

fisherman's clams

1.8kg (4lb) clams or any fresh shellfish

2 tablespoons olive oil

2 garlic cloves, finely chopped

1 green frying chilli, deseeded and chopped

1 fresh red chilli, deseeded and finely chopped

1 tablespoon chopped parsley

Pick over the clams and rinse thoroughly. Heat the oil in a roomy pan and fry the garlic and chillies for 2-3 minutes, just enough to perfume the oil. Tip in the shellfish, turn up the heat and bubble for 3-4 minutes, until all the shells gape open in the steam – turn them with a spoon so that the ones on top can get to the heat. When all are open, they're done. Remove the pan from the heat immediately – shellfish toughens if it's overcooked. Finish with freshly chopped parsley.

TIP

Leave the clams to soak overnight in cold water and discard any with cracked or gaping shells and those which feel too heavy - a sign they're full of something other than live fish. Shellfish can stay fresh for as long as they can hold water in their shells.

Nutritional value per serving:

Calories: 134

Fats: 7g

Carbohydrates: 1g

Salt: 0.19g

Saturated fat: 1g

Fibre: 0.2g

stir-fried crab claws with spring onion, chilli & garlic

Chilli paste

1 red chilli, deseeded and finely chopped

2 cloves garlic, chopped

1cm ($^1\!/_2$in) root ginger, peeled and chopped

$1^1\!/_2$ tablespoons rice wine vinegar

1 tablespoon caster sugar

$^1\!/_2$ teaspoon sea salt

125ml (4fl oz) vegetable oil

1 tablespoon chilli paste

50g (2oz) root ginger, peeled and sliced

4 crab claws, boiled, shell cracked and cleaned

2 tablespoons *nam pla* (Thai fish sauce)

4 spring onions, thinly sliced, green parts
   reserved for garnish

freshly ground black pepper

coriander leaves, to garnish

To make the chilli paste: Blend the chilli, garlic and ginger in a food processor until it forms a rough paste. Add the rice wine vinegar, sugar and salt and mix well.

Heat the vegetable oil in a wok over a medium heat. Add the chilli paste and stir-fry for 1-2 minutes. Add the ginger and crab claws. Stir in the fish sauce and add the spring onions. Toss well, reduce the heat and place a lid or a piece of foil on top. Cook for 2-3 minutes, shaking the wok. Season with black pepper and serve immediately, garnished with spring onion strips and coriander leaves.

Nutritional value per serving:

Calories: 662

Fats: 64g

Carbohydrates: 7g

Salt: 3.87g

Saturated fat: 7.2g

Fibre: 0.3g

squid with dry curry

175-225g (6-8oz) squid (bodies only), washed
  and cleaned

2 tablespoons vegetable oil

2 garlic cloves, finely chopped

2 teaspoons red curry paste

1 tablespoon *nam pla* (Thai fish sauce)

1 tablespoon light soy sauce

1 teaspoon granulated sugar

2-3 small green aubergines, quartered

1 small fresh red chilli, finely chopped

2 kaffir lime leaves, finely sliced

10 fresh holy basil leaves

Score the squid finely on both sides, then cut into pieces about 2.5cm (1in) square. Set aside. In a wok or frying pan, heat the oil and fry the garlic until golden brown. Stir in the curry paste and cook for a few seconds. Add the squid, coating it in the sauce. Add the fish sauce, soy sauce, sugar and aubergines and stir-fry over a high heat until the aubergines are cooked through. Now stir in the chilli, lime leaves and basil.

When the squid is cooked through and opaque, give the dish a final stir and pour into a serving dish.

How to prepare squid

Cut off the tentacles then pull the entrails out of the sac and discard. Remove the 'beak' and pull the quill out of the sac. Pull off the wings and scrape the purplish membrane off them and the sac. Cut the body into rings.

Nutritional value per serving:

Calories: 110

Fats: 7g

Carbohydrates: 4g

Salt: 1.58g

Saturated fat: 0.7g

Fibre: 1.1g

seared fillet of salmon with new potatoes & citrus salad

16 small new potatoes, scrubbed clean

3 oranges, segmented as shown below, juice reserved

3 lemons, segmented as shown below, juice reserved

About 125ml (4fl oz) olive oil

4 salmon fillets, skinned

4 tablespoons chopped fresh coriander

200g (7oz) rocket leaves

Boil the potatoes in salted water for 12-15 minutes until just tender. Drain, allow to cool a little and slice. Season and drizzle over a little of the olive oil. Place the orange and lemon segments in a separate bowl. Add 100ml (3½fl oz) of the olive oil to the juices and whisk together to combine, then season to taste. Heat a non-stick frying pan and add the remaining olive oil. Season the salmon fillets and add to the pan and cook for 3-4 minutes until seared and lightly golden. Turn over and cook for another minute until just tender. Transfer to a plate and keep warm. Tip the orange and lemon segments into the dressing and then add the coriander and rocket leaves, tossing to combine. Arrange the salmon fillets on serving plates and place the new potatoes on the side with the rocket salad on top.

How to segment citrus fruit

Use a sharp knife to cut off the top and bottom of the fruit, then peel the skin and pith in a spiral. Cut in front of each membrane towards the centre of the fruit then push the knife forward to remove the segment cleanly. Continue all around the fruit.

Nutritional value per serving:

Calories: 644

Fats: 45g

Carbohydrates: 29g

Salt: 0.22g

Saturated fat: 7.1g

Fibre: 3.9g

medallion of **monkfish** with soy & choy sum

900g (2lb) choy sum (available from Asian
   markets), shredded
juice of 1 lemon
5 cloves garlic, crushed
2.5cm (1in) root ginger, peeled and grated
2 tablespoons sweet soy sauce
1 tablespoon olive oil
900g (2lb) monkfish fillets, cut into 12
   medallions
1 carrot, cut into thin strips
4 spring onions, cut into thin strips
50g (2oz) butter, cubed
1 large red chilli pepper, deseeded and cut
   into strips
salt and freshly ground black pepper

Blanch the choy sum in a pan of boiling, salted water for 3 minutes and refresh under cold water. Drain well. Rinse out the pan.

Combine the lemon juice, garlic, grated ginger and soy sauce in a bowl.

Place the oil in the pan over a high heat and cook the monkfish for 1 minute on each side. Add the choy sum, carrot and spring onions, and the garlic mixture. Increase the heat and add the butter. Swirl the pan to incorporate the butter, season well and sprinkle with the chilli strips. Serve immediately.

TIP

This dish is a good source of iron, folic acid as well as Vitamins A and C.

Nutritional value per serving:
Calories: 352
Fats: 15g
Carbohydrates: 12g
Salt: 3.31g
Saturated fat: 7.2g
Fibre: 0.9g

grilled john dory on the bone

4 very fresh whole John Dory

salt and freshly ground pepper

butter, for frying

50-110g (2-4oz) butter

4 teaspoons mixed fresh parsley, chives, fennel
and thyme leaves, finely chopped

Remove the head from the fish. Score the skin crossways on both sides, sprinkle with a little salt and pepper and spread butter on both sides of the fish. Grill for 10-12 minutes at a medium heat; you will need to turn the fish once during the cooking time, which will depend on the size or thickness of the fish. Meanwhile, melt the butter and stir in the freshly chopped herbs. Spoon the herb butter over the fish and serve immediately.

How to chop fresh herbs

Wash and dry the herbs, discarding the stalks or saving them for the stockpot. Gather the herbs into a little ball and chop roughly. Change the angle of the knife to a horizontal position and rock the blade backwards and forwards until the herbs are chopped finely.

Nutritional value per serving:

Calories: 317

Fats: 14g

Carbohydrates: 0g

Salt: 0.87g

Saturated fat: 7.2g

Fibre: 0.1g

baked **mackerel** with carrot noodles

4 large carrots

4 x 225g (8oz) mackerel

1 teaspoon coriander seeds, crushed

2 shallots, finely diced

zest of 1 orange, grated

2 tablespoons fresh coriander leaves, finely
   chopped

1 tablespoon balsamic vinegar

2 tablespoons extra-virgin olive oil

salt and freshly ground black pepper

Using a potato peeler, shave the carrots into noodles. Season the mackerel fillets with salt, pepper and the crushed coriander seeds. Place on a baking tray skin-side up and bake in a pre-heated oven at 230°C/450°F/gas mark 8 for 10 minutes.

Meanwhile, bring a saucepan of salted water to the boil and blanch the carrot noodles for a couple of seconds, then refresh under cold running water and drain well.

In a bowl mix together the shallots, orange zest, coriander leaves, vinegar, oil and seasoning. When the fish is ready, arrange the noodles on a serving plate and season with a little of the dressing. Place the fish fillets on top, spoon over the remaining dressing and serve.

Nutritional value per serving:

Calories: 475

Fats: 34g

Carbohydrates: 9g

Salt: 0.34g

Saturated fat: 6.1g

Fibre: 2.2g

red mullet in a parcel

6 pieces of silver foil measuring 20 x 20cm
   (8 x 8in)
3 tablespoons olive oil
1 medium fennel, sliced across thinly
1 medium onion, sliced into thin rings
6 red mullets, cleaned and washed
a few sprigs of thyme
2 cloves of garlic, sliced thinly
6 thin slices of lemon
salt and freshly ground black pepper
lemon wedges, to serve

Preheat the oven to 200°C/400°F/gas mark 6.

Oil the centre of each foil square generously (this will use roughly half the oil) and distribute the sliced fennel and onion evenly.

Stuff the cavity of each fish with a sprig of thyme and the garlic and lay them on top of the vegetables. Sprinkle with the rest of the oil. Lay a slice of lemon on each, season with salt and pepper and parcel up tightly. Bake in the preheated oven for 10-15 minutes, opening the parcels for the last 5 minutes.

When the fish is nicely browned, serve decorated with lemon wedges. If more salt is needed, sprinkle with a bit of coarse sea salt.

Nutritional value per serving:
Calories: 292
Fats: 15g
Carbohydrates: 4g
Salt: 0.68g
Saturated fat: 3.2g
Fibre: 1.3g

steamed fish with chilli paste

2 long dried red chillies, deseeded and soaked
  in water to soften

3 garlic cloves, chopped

3 small red shallots, chopped

2.5cm (1in) piece of galangal, peeled and
  coarsely chopped

1 tablespoon chopped lemongrass

450g (1lb) monkfish (or another freshwater
  fish), filleted and cut into 2.5cm (1in) chunks

2 tablespoons *nam pla* (Thai fish sauce)

2 fresh sweet basil leaves

Using a pestle and mortar, pound together the chillies, garlic, shallots, galangal and lemongrass to make a paste.

Place the fish pieces in a mixing bowl with the fish sauce, basil leaves and paste and mix gently together.

Place the mixture in a heatproof bowl and steam for 15 minutes. Serve in the bowl.

TIP

Galangal is a creamy-white rhizome and is slightly harder than ginger. It is used in the same way, but has a more lemony flavour.

Nutritional value per serving:

Calories: 89

Fats: 1g

Carbohydrates: 3g

Salt: 1.42g

Saturated fat: 0.1g

Fibre: 0.3g

grilled **tuna** with salsa verde

4 x 200g (7oz) tuna steaks
olive oil, for brushing
1 lemon, quartered, to serve

Salsa verde
1 garlic clove
bunch of flat-leaf parsley, chopped
1 spring onion, finely chopped
2 anchovy fillets, finely chopped
1 teaspoon Dijon mustard
1 dessertspoon capers
4 tablespoons olive oil
salt and freshly ground black pepper

Preheat a hot grill.

Make the salsa verde: finely chop the garlic and crush it with a little salt. Work all the ingredients except the oil in a mortar with a pestle until they form a rough paste. Whisk in the olive oil (you may need a little more) until the sauce has a thick consistency. Adjust the seasoning.

Lightly brush the tuna with olive oil, season well with salt and pepper and grill for 2 minutes each side.

Serve each tuna steak with a generous spoonful of the salsa and a lemon quarter.

Nutritional value per serving:
Calories: 394
Fats: 22g
Carbohydrates: 1g
Salt: 0.89g
Saturated fat: 4.8g
Fibre: 0.3g

SERVES 4

PREPARATION TIME: 10 MINUTES

COOKING TIME: 35 MINUTES

baked stuffed trout

4 tablespoons extra-virgin olive oil

1 small onion, finely chopped

1 garlic clove, finely chopped

1 teaspoon paprika

1 teaspoon cayenne pepper

220g (8oz) canned chopped tomatoes

200g (7oz) canned chickpeas, drained

4 large sprigs flat-leaf parsley, finely chopped

juice of 1 large lemon

4 small salmon trout, trimmed and gutted

150ml (5fl oz) dry white wine

50g (2oz) unsalted butter

salt and freshly ground black pepper

Preheat the oven to 220°C/425°F/gas mark 7.

Heat the oil in a frying pan, add the onions and garlic, and sweat gently for 5 minutes. Stir in the paprika and cayenne pepper and cook for a further 2 minutes. Add the tomatoes and chickpeas and simmer until tender – about 10 minutes.

Mash the mixture roughly, pouring off any excess tomato juice until you have the consistency of a stuffing. Add the parsley and lemon juice and mix into the stuffing. Pile the stuffing into the trout cavities.

Cut 4 pieces of kitchen foil big enough to totally envelope each fish. Put each trout on a piece of foil. Divide the wine among them, season, dot with the butter and seal the parcels. Bake for 20 minutes. Open the foil carefully to let the steam escape before serving.

Nutritional value per serving:

Calories: 476

Fats: 29g

Carbohydrates: 9g

Salt: 0.55g

Saturated fat: 9.7g

Fibre: 2.1g

chicken tortillas with avocado, chilli & soured cream

400g (14oz) boneless, skinless chicken, diced

2 tablespoons olive oil

4 soft flour tortillas, each about 20cm (8in) in diameter

2 ripe avocados

2 heaped tablespoons soured cream

1 ripe tomato, peeled, deseeded and diced

1 red chilli, deseeded and finely chopped

Preheat the grill or a griddle pan. Thread the chicken on to soaked wooden skewers, making sure they are not too tightly packed together. Brush with the olive oil and cook for 4-5 minutes, depending on the size of the dice or until the chicken is completely tender and lightly charred. Leave until cool enough to handle.

Place the tortillas on the grill rack and then place under the grill for 30 seconds to 1 minute to just warm through, turning once. Alternatively, use the griddle pan.

Meanwhile, remove the chicken from the skewers. Peel the avocados and then cut each one in half and remove the stones. Cut the flesh into 1cm ($^1/_2$in) dice. Spread the softened tortillas with the soured cream and scatter the chicken down the centre of each one. Place the avocado on top with the tomato dice and chilli, then roll up to enclose the filling completely.

Return to the grill rack and place under the grill, seam-side down for 1-2 minutes until the tops are lightly toasted; or use the griddle pan. Cut each tortilla in half on the diagonal and arrange on warmed serving plates. Serve immediately.

Nutritional value per serving:

Calories: 480

Fats: 25g

Carbohydrates: 35g

Salt: 0.6g

Saturated fat: 5g

Fibre: 4g

TIP

Keep a packet of flour tortillas in the cupboard - they often come in handy. To make them soft enough for rolling, place them under the grill or on a frying or griddle pan. Alternatively, they can also be microwaved on high between dampened sheets of kitchen paper for about 20 seconds.

SERVES 8

PREPARATION TIME: 10 MINUTES

COOKING TIME: 10 MINUTES

MARINATING TIME: 2 HOURS

pan-grilled chicken breasts with cardamom

8 chicken breasts

1 teaspoon cardamom seeds

1 teaspoon black peppercorns

good pinch cayenne pepper

4 tablespoons olive oil

50g (2oz) butter

finely grated rind and juice of 1 lemon

Flatten the chicken breasts slightly. Pound the cardamom and peppercorns together in a mortar and add the cayenne and olive oil. Dip the chicken breasts in this marinade, cover and leave to marinade for about 2 hours.

Pan-grill the chicken breasts or barbecue them on an oiled rack about 12.5cm (5in) from the coals, cook for several minutes each side, brushing with extra marinade while cooking. Cream the butter, add the finely grated lemon rind and beat in the juice very gradually.

Spoon the butter over the chicken breasts and serve with a good green salad.

Nutritional value per serving:

Calories: 249

Fats: 12g

Carbohydrates: 1g

Salt: 0.33g

Saturated fat: 4.5g

Fibre: 0g

whole boneless quail with peaches

4 whole boneless oven-ready quail

25g (1oz) light muscovado sugar

8 ripe peaches, halved and stoned

600ml (1 pint) muscat wine

2 vanilla pods, split

2 head of Swiss chard, cut into julienne as
shown below

Preheat the oven to 200°C/400°F/gas mark 6. Place the quails in the centre of a large ovenproof dish, using cocktail sticks to help keep them in shape. Roast in the oven for 3-5 minutes until golden brown, then drizzle with olive oil and season to taste. Return to the oven and cook for another minute or two or until the juices just begin to run. Remove from the oven and sprinkle the sugar over the quails. Surround with the peaches and pour in the muscat wine. Tuck in the vanilla pods and sprinkle the Swiss chard julienne on top. Return to oven and cook for another 5-7 minutes or until the quails are completely tender. Bring the dish straight to the table and serve in warmed wide-rimmed bowls.

TIP

Boneless quail are available in most major supermarkets or you could always try and get your butcher to prepare them for you – just give some advance notice.

How to julienne Swiss chard

Wash and dry the leaves. Remove the midribs with a sharp knife. (Use them for another recipe.) Roll up each leaf tightly and cut each roll into fine slices.

Nutritional value per serving:

Calories: 526

Fats: 14g

Carbohydrates: 35g

Salt: 0.48g

Saturated fat: 3.4g

Fibre: 3.3g

vietnamese pork & lemongrass patties

450g (1lb) lean, minced pork

25g (1oz) shallots, chopped

2 stalks lemongrass, trimmed and very finely chopped

$1/2$ teaspoon salt

lots of freshly ground black pepper

Put everything into a food processor, season well with salt and pepper, and whizz for just a few seconds. Heat a frying pan and cook a tiny piece to check the seasoning, adjusting if necessary.

Make the meat mixture into patties up to 8cm (3in) in diameter and pan-grill for 5 minutes on each side. Or you can make the meat into small balls about 5cm (2in) in diameter and thread them onto well-soaked bamboo skewers and barbecue them for 10-15 minutes, turning on all sides.

Nutritional value per serving:

Calories: 143

Fats: 5g

Carbohydrates: 1g

Salt: 0.81g

Saturated fat: 1.5g

Fibre: 0.1g

calves' liver with almonds

leaves of 1 large sprig rosemary, finely chopped

2 garlic cloves, very finely chopped

110g (4oz) fresh wholemeal breadcrumbs

110g (4oz) ground almonds

2 pinches ground saffron

4 tablespoons extra-virgin olive oil

50g (2oz) unsalted butter

4 x 175g (6oz) slices calves' liver

150ml (5fl oz) red wine

110g (4oz) raisins

freshly ground black pepper

steamed carrots and broccoli, to serve

Mix the rosemary, garlic, breadcrumbs, almonds and saffron into half the oil. Season with black pepper.

Heat the butter and remaining oil in a large frying pan. Add the liver and cook for 3-4 minutes, depending on thickness and how pink you like it, turning once. Remove and keep warm.

Put all the other ingredients into the pan and boil briskly for 2 minutes, stirring to loosen any liver stuck to the bottom.

Serve the liver with the sauce spooned over the top and accompanied by steamed carrots and broccoli.

TIP

This dish is packed with goodness - iron, zinc and folic acid as well as Vitamins A, B6 and C. Pregnant or breastfeeding women are advised to limit their consumption of liver to one portion per week.

Nutritional value per serving:

Calories: 707

Fats: 43g

Carbohydrates: 33g

Salt: 0.76g

Saturated fat: 11.3g

Fibre: 4.3g

lamb steaks with fresh apricot sauce

2 tablespoons honey

2 tablespoons olive oil

4-6 x 150g (6oz) lamb steaks

salt and freshly ground black pepper

Apricot sauce

450g (1lb) fresh apricots, kernels removed, or
    150g (6oz) dried apricots

1-2 tablespoons honey, to taste

2 tablespoons chopped mint (or 1 tablespoon
    dried)

few drops of lemon juice

$1/2$ teaspoon grated lemon zest

salt and freshly ground black pepper

Heat the grill to maximum. Mix the honey with the oil and brush over the steaks. Season with salt and pepper. Grill at a high heat for 4-5 minutes each side. this will result in a medium-rare lamb steak; if you like your lamb well done, grill for a few minutes more.

Put all the sauce ingredients into a food processor and process to a smooth puree.

Decorate each steak with a sprig of mint and serve on a pool of sauce.

Nutritional value per serving:

Calories: 355

Fats: 18g

Carbohydrates: 17g

Salt: 0.78g

Saturated fat: 6.7g

Fibre: 2g

marinated sirloin skewers

1 onion, thinly sliced

50g (2oz) fresh root ginger, peeled and cut into
julienne (see below)

125ml (4fl oz) dark soy sauce

450g (1lb) sirloin steak, cut into 2.5cm (1in)
cubes

4 tablespoons olive oil

110g (4oz) shiitake mushrooms, sliced

2 carrots, peeled and cut into julienne

Place the onion, ginger and soy sauce in a shallow non-metallic dish. Add the steak cubes, stirring to combine, then cover with cling film and chill for at least 3 hours, or overnight.

Heat a large non-stick frying pan until hot. Drain the beef from the marinade, reserving it to use later, then thread the beef on to 8 x 15cm (6in) wooden skewers. Add the oil to the pan and when the oil begins to smoke, sear the skewers on all sides – you may have to do this in two batches, depending on the size of your pan. Transfer to a warmed plate and keep warm.

Add the mushrooms and carrots to the same pan that you have cooked the beef in, then sauté for 2 minutes. Add four tablespoons of the reserved marinade, reduce the heat and continue to cook for about 1 minute, stirring occasionally. Arrange the skewers on warmed serving plates with the vegetables and spoon over any remaining sauce. Serve at once.

How to julienne vegetables

Wash and peel the vegetable. Square off the sides (saving the trimmings for the stockpot) and cut the vegetables crossways into 5cm (2in) lengths. Cut lengthways into thin slices then stack and cut lengthways into thin strips.

Nutritional value per serving:

Calories: 313

Fats: 17g

Carbohydrates: 12g

Salt: 5.94g

Saturated fat: 3.6g

Fibre: 1.5g

beef & vegetable noodles with black beans

2 tablespoons vegetable oil

225g (8oz) cooked egg noodles, drained and
  separated

1 tablespoon light soy sauce

1 garlic clove, finely chopped

110g (4oz) beef steak, finely sliced

1 tablespoon *nam pla* (Thai fish sauce)

4 tablespoons beef stock, plus extra if necessary

1 teaspoon black bean sauce

1 teaspoon plain flour mixed with 4 tablespoons
  water to make a thin paste (this will give
  more than you need)

110g (4oz) mixed green vegetables (spring
  greens, mangetout, broccoli, for example)

1/2 teaspoon granulated sugar

1/4 teaspoon ground white pepper

In a wok or frying pan, heat 1 tablespoon oil. Add the noodles and stir-fry quickly to prevent them from sticking. Add the soy sauce and stir-fry for 30-60 seconds. Turn on to a serving dish, keep warm and set aside.

Add the remaining oil to the wok and fry the garlic until golden brown. Add the beef and stir-fry over a high heat until the meat loses its red colour. Stir in the fish sauce, a little stock and the black bean sauce. Thicken with a little of the flour and water mixture, stirring all the time to prevent lumps forming. Toss in the vegetables and sugar and stir-fry for a few seconds. Season with pepper, stir once, then pour over the noodles and serve.

Nutritional value per serving:

Calories: 140

Fats: 7g

Carbohydrates: 11g

Salt: 1.55g

Saturated fat: 1.2g

Fibre: 1.1g

okra and bean stew

4 corn on the cob, husks removed

50g (2oz) unsalted butter

350g (12oz) small okra (ladies' fingers),
  trimmed

4 spring onions, shredded

$1/2$ red pepper, cut into small dice

$1/2$ green pepper, cut into small dice

$1/2$ garlic clove, crushed

$1/2$ teaspoon dried thyme

$1/2$ teaspoon ground paprika

$1/2$ teaspoon ground cumin

400g (14oz) can of butter beans

$1^1/2$ teaspoons lemon juice

salt and freshly ground black pepper

Using a small knife, shuck the corn kernels into a bowl along with any juices from the corn, as shown below.

Dice half the butter and chill it. Heat the remaining butter in a large frying pan, add the okra, spring onions and peppers and cook over a moderate heat for 3-4 minutes. Add the shucked corn, garlic, thyme and spices, lower the heat and cook until fragrant, about 4-5 minutes. Add the canned beans and their liquid, stirring them in to heat through. Season to taste, stir in the lemon juice and then whisk in the reserved butter a few pieces at a time.

TIP

This vegetarian dish is a valuable source of iron, calcium, folic acid and fibre, as well as Vitamins A, B6 and C. Butter beans provide low-fat protein.

How to remove corn kernels

Remove the husks and the silky threads from the corn cobs. Hold each cob upright on a work surface and cut off the kernels with a sharp knife.

Nutritional value per serving:

Calories: 275

Fats: 14g

Carbohydrates: 30g

Salt: 0.89g

Saturated fat: 6.5g

Fibre: 8.4g

salads, soups & side dishes

cabbage & beetroot soup

4 tablespoons rapeseed oil

1 onion, finely chopped

1 garlic clove, finely chopped

450g (1lb) raw baby beetroot, diced

1 litre ($1^3/_4$ pints) vegetable stock

2 tablespoons cider vinegar

275g (10oz) white cabbage, coarsely shredded
   (see page 154)

8 chives

Heat the oil in a large saucepan, add the onion and garlic, and sweat gently for 5 minutes.

Mix in the beetroot, pour in the stock and boil until tender. Whizz in a blender with the cider vinegar and return to the saucepan.

Scatter the cabbage on the soup, but don't stir. Cover and boil gently for 5 minutes, until the cabbage is almost cooked but still crunchy.

Serve with chives arranged on top.

Nutritional value per serving:

Calories: 178

Fats: 11g

Carbohydrates: 15g

Salt: 1.03g

Saturated fat: 0.8g

Fibre: 4.1g

mussel soup with fine beans, tomato & coriander

1.5kg (3lb 5oz) mussels, cleaned and debearded
   (see page 64)
300ml (1/2 pint) dry white wine
3 tablespoons olive oil
1 onion, finely chopped
200g (7oz) fine green beans, finely chopped
3 plum tomatoes, peeled, seeded and diced
1 bunch of fresh coriander, leaves stripped and
   chopped
white peppercorns (optional)

Prepare the mussels, discarding any that won't close when they are lightly tapped on the work surface.

Heat a large pan over a high heat. Tip in the mussels and cover for 10-15 seconds, then pour over the wine and 300ml (1/2 pint) of water. Add a few white peppercorns if you've got them, then cover and cook, shaking the pan every now and then, for 5 minutes or until all the mussels have opened. Discard any that stay closed.

Tip the mussels into a colander set over a large bowl and then pass the cooking liquid once more through a fine sieve and reserve. When the mussels are cool enough to handle, remove the mussel meats from their shells and reserve, discarding the shells.

Heat a pan. Add one tablespoon of the olive oil and then add the onion. Cook for a few minutes until softened, then pour in the reserved cooking liquid and bring to the boil. Season to taste. Add the beans, mussels and tomatoes and just warm through. Ladle into warmed wide-rimmed bowls, scatter over the coriander and drizzle over the remaining olive oil. Serve immediately.

Nutritional value per serving:
Calories: 245
Fats: 11g
Carbohydrates: 10g
Salt: 0.86g
Saturated fat: 1.5g
Fibre: 2.4g

chilled avocado soup

5 ripe avocados, peeled and stoned

1 litre (1$^3/_4$ pints) chicken stock

juice of 1 large lemon

2 large garlic cloves, finely chopped

3 red chillies, deseeded and chopped

$^1/_4$ teaspoon cayenne pepper

4 plump spring onions, roughly chopped

leaves of 12 large stems coriander

200g (7oz) canned organic plum tomatoes, drained

150ml (5fl oz) natural organic bio-yogurt

4 tablespoons pumpkin seeds

salt and freshly ground black pepper

Put the avocado flesh into a food processor with the chicken stock and add the lemon juice.

Add the garlic, chillies and cayenne pepper and blend smooth.

Add the spring onions, coriander leaves and tomatoes, and process briefly again.

Add the yogurt and whizz for just a few seconds. Adjust the seasoning and leave in the fridge to chill.

Nutritional value per serving:

Calories: 450

Fats: 41g

Carbohydrates: 10g

Salt: 1.22g

Saturated fat: 6g

Fibre: 6.9g

spiced gazpacho

1/2 small cucumber

450g (1lb) good quality fresh tomatoes

1/2 red onion

1/2 yellow pepper, cored and seeded

1 garlic clove, crushed

1 red chilli, seeded and finely chopped

1 small handful parsley

1 small handful coriander

1 dessertspoon extra-virgin olive oil

pinch of paprika

1 tablespoon cider vinegar

sea salt and freshly ground black pepper

parsley and coriander leaves, to garnish

Place all ingredients except the herbs for garnishing in a food processor and blend until the mixture is well chopped, but not puréed. Serve at room temperature, garnished.

Nutritional value per serving:

Calories: 115

Fats: 6g

Carbohydrates: 14g

Salt: 0.32g

Saturated fat: 0.7g

Fibre: 4.1g

chilled asparagus & lemon soup

275g (10oz) asparagus, trimmed and peeled
125ml (4fl oz) vegetable stock or water
1 small onion, finely chopped
1 medium potato, peeled and diced
800ml ($1^1/_3$ pints) water
2 tablespoons chopped oregano
juice of 1 lemon
salt and freshly ground black pepper
lemon zest, to garnish

Cut off the tips of the asparagus and reserve. Cut the rest into thin strips 2-3cm ($^3/_4$-$1^1/_4$in) long. Heat the stock in a pan, add the onion, cover and simmer gently for 5 minutes. Add the potato to the pan with the asparagus strips and water, bring to the boil and simmer for 10 minutes, until the potato and asparagus are very soft. Add the oregano and lemon juice to the pan and simmer for 2-3 minutes, then blend in a liquidiser or food processor.

Steam the asparagus tips for 2-3 minutes until just tender and add to the smooth soup. Season to taste, chill and serve garnished.

Nutritional value per serving:
Calories: 72
Fats: 1g
Carbohydrates: 12g
Salt: 0.43g
Saturated fat: 0g
Fibre: 2.7g

orange, carrot & ginger soup

1 medium onion, finely chopped

3 medium carrots, peeled and finely sliced

350ml (12fl oz) vegetable stock

5cm (2in) root ginger, peeled and finely grated

350ml (12fl oz) water

zest of $\frac{1}{2}$ orange

juice of 1 orange

sea salt and freshly ground black pepper

chopped chives, to garnish

Place the onion, carrots and stock in a large pan, bring to the boil and simmer for 15 minutes. Gather the grated ginger into your hand and squeeze the juice into the soup. Discard the ginger fibre. Add the water, orange juice and zest to the pan, bring back to the boil and simmer for another 10 minutes. Remove the pan from the heat and allow the soup to cool slightly before blending in a food processor or liquidiser until smooth. Reheat and serve garnished with chives.

Nutritional value per serving:

Calories: 89

Fats: 1g

Carbohydrates: 19g

Salt: 0.9g

Saturated fat: 0.1g

Fibre: 4.2g

tomato salad

8-12 tomatoes: use one variety, or a mixture, of
   very ripe red or yellow vine-ripened tomatoes
extra-virgin olive oil
2-4 teaspoons basil leaves or mint leaves
sea salt, freshly ground pepper and sugar

Dressing
75ml (3fl oz) olive oil or a mixture of olive and
   other oils e.g. sunflower and groundnut
25ml (1fl oz) white wine vinegar
$\frac{1}{2}$ level teaspoon mustard (Dijon or English)
$\frac{1}{2}$ level teaspoon salt
few grinds of black pepper
1 garlic clove, peeled (and mashed if not using
   a blender)
sprig of parsley
1 small spring onion
sprig of watercress

First, make the dressing: put all the ingredients into a blender and run at medium speed for about 1 minute, or mix oil and vinegar in a bowl and add mustard, salt, pepper and garlic. Chop the parsley, spring onion and watercress finely and add in. Whisk before serving.

Cut the tomatoes in half or lengthways or into wedges, or simply into 1cm ($\frac{1}{2}$in) thick slices depending on shape and size.

Spread out in a single layer on a large flat plate, season with salt, pepper and a sprinkling of sugar. Sprinkle with dressing. Scatter with torn basil or mint leaves. Toss gently, just to coat the tomatoes. Serve soon either as a first course or as an accompanying salad.

TIP

Tomatoes must be dressed as soon as they are cut to seal in their flavour.

Nutritional value per serving:
Calories: 188
Fats: 18g
Carbohydrates: 6g
Salt: 0.96g
Saturated fat: 2.4g
Fibre: 1.8g

avocado & strawberry salad

1 ripe avocado, halved, stoned, peeled and cut
   into cubes
6 strawberries, hulled and quartered
2 teaspoons lemon juice
2 teaspoons balsamic vinegar
salt and freshly ground black pepper

Place the avocado in a bowl with the strawberries. Mix together the lemon juice and vinegar, pour over the salad and mix gently. Season to taste and serve immediately.

Nutritional value per serving:
Calories: 148
Fats: 14g
Carbohydrates: 5g
Salt: 0.52g
Saturated fat: 1.6g
Fibre: 2.8g

spiced yogurt relish

1 red onion, thinly sliced

1 cucumber, halved, deseeded and thinly sliced

1 teaspoon toasted cumin seeds

bunch of coriander, roughly chopped (stems
and all)

2 tomatoes, quartered, deseeded and thinly
sliced

400ml (14fl oz) plain full-fat runny yogurt

salt and freshly ground black pepper

Combine the onion and cucumber in a sieve, sprinkle liberally with salt and set over a bowl for 10 minutes. Rinse thoroughly and pat dry – this should rid the cucumber of some of its water and the onion of some of its strength.

Combine the onion and cucumber with the cumin seeds, coriander, tomatoes and yogurt. Stir well and adjust the seasoning (carefully, as there is probably enough salt from the cucumber and onion).

Nutritional value per rounded tablespoon:

Calories: 19

Fats: 0g

Carbohydrates: 3g

Salt: 0.1g

Saturated fat: 0.2g

Fibre: 0.3g

moroccan lemon salad

4 ripe, thin-skinned lemons

2 teaspoons olive oil

2 teaspoons or more harissa, to taste

1 bunch flat-leaf parsley, chopped

Slice the lemons into thin rounds, discarding any pips. Add the rest of the ingredients and mix well.

TIP

You can peel the lemons if you don't like things too bitter.

Nutritional value per serving:

Calories: 40

Fats: 3g

Carbohydrates: 3g

Salt: 0.04g

Saturated fat: 0.02g

Fibre: 0.2g

papaya salad

2 garlic cloves, peeled

3-4 small fresh red or green chillies

2 yard-long beans or 20 French beans, chopped
   into 5cm (2in) lengths

175g (6oz) fresh papaya, peeled, deseeded and
   cut into fine slivers

1 tomato, cut into wedges

2 tablespoons *nam pla* (Thai fish sauce)

1 tablespoon granulated sugar

2 tablespoons lime juice

a selection of fresh firm green vegetables in
   season e.g. iceberg lettuce, cucumber, white
   cabbage - to serve

Pound the garlic in a large mortar, then add the chillies and pound again. Add the long beans, breaking them up slightly. Now take a spoon and stir in the papaya. Lightly pound together, then stir in the tomato and lightly pound again.

Add the fish sauce, sugar and lime juice, stirring well, then turn into a serving dish. Serve with fresh raw vegetables – any leaves, such as white cabbage, can be used as a scoop for the spicy mixture.

TIP

As the name suggests, yard-long beans are an extra-long variety of green beans often used in Asian cookery. If you can't find them, use ordinary green beans instead.

Nutritional value per serving:

Calories: 51

Fats: 0g

Carbohydrates: 11g

Salt: 1.37g

Saturated fat: 0g

Fibre: 2.1g

raw artichoke salad

4 large artichokes, cleaned as below

1 bunch spring onions

2 large tomatoes, peeled, deseeded and roughly
    chopped

3 tablespoons virgin olive oil

juice of 1 lemon or to taste

1 clove of garlic, finely chopped

$^1/_2$ lemon sliced into thin slices, each slice cut
    into small wedges

3 tablespoons parsley, roughly chopped

salt and freshly ground black pepper

Prepare the artichokes as shown below.

Combine the rest of the ingredients in a large salad bowl and mix well. Slice the artichoke hearts into thin crescents and immediately coat with the dressing. Decorate with artichoke leaves and serve.

TIP

This salad improves if left to marinate for a few hours. The artichoke hearts will not discolour once they are coated in the dressing.

How to prepare artichoke hearts

Cut the leaves off halfway down the artichoke, exposing the choky heart. Continue to trim off the leaves carefully until you are left with just the heart and the choke. With a sharp knife scrape away the choke. Immediately plunge the peeled artichoke into cold acidulated water (with lemon juice added) as the cut surface blackens very quickly. Do not throw away the leaves, use to decorate the salad.

Nutritional value per serving:

Calories: 155

Fats: 9g

Carbohydrates: 10g

Salt: 0.44g

Saturated fat: 1.2g

Fibre: 1.2g

aubergine, basil, spinach & chilli salad

2 aubergines

large handful of basil leaves

3 tablespoons olive oil

4 tomatoes, sliced

225g (8oz) baby spinach

1 garlic clove

200ml (7fl oz) yogurt

1 red chilli, deseeded and finely chopped

1 heaped tablespoon pine nuts

juice of 1 lemon

salt and freshly ground black pepper

good bread, to serve

Preheat a hot grill and cook the aubergines as shown below. Transfer to a bowl and cover with cling film. If working in batches, make sure to cover the bowl again each time.

Roughly chop the basil leaves and add these to the bowl, together with the olive oil, tomatoes and spinach leaves. Mash the garlic with $1/2$ teaspoon of salt, whisk this into the yogurt and add the mixture to the aubergine together with the chilli. Heat a dry frying pan and, when hot, toast the pine nuts until they just begin to colour. Add these to the bowl. Toss everything well together, squeeze over the juice of the lemon and serve with lots of good bread.

TIP

This salad is a good source of calcium, folic acid, fibre and Vitamins A, C and E.

How to chargrill aubergines

Slice the aubergines lengthways into 1cm ($1/2$in) slices. Heat a ridged grill pan over a high heat and brush the aubergine slices (not the grill) with olive oil. Grill for 2-3 minutes on each side until soft and charred.

Nutritional value per serving:

Calories: 194

Fats: 14g

Carbohydrates: 11g

Salt: 0.58g

Saturated fat: 2g

Fibre: 5.2g

tabbouleh

110g (4oz) bulgur (cracked wheat)

75ml (3fl oz) extra virgin olive oil

juice of 2 organic lemons or more if you need
it, freshly squeezed

25-50g (1-2oz) parsley, freshly chopped

25-50g (1-2oz) mint, freshly chopped

50-110g (2-4oz) spring onion, green and white
parts, chopped

salt and freshly ground pepper

To serve

small crisp lettuce leaves (cos or iceberg)

6 very ripe firm tomatoes, (a selection of red
and yellow looks great), deseeded, diced and
sprinkled with a little salt, pepper and sugar

1 firm crisp cucumber, cut into 5mm (¼in) dice

rocket leaves or flat-leaf parsley

black olives (optional)

Soak the bulgur in cold water for about 30 minutes, drain and squeeze well to remove any excess water. Stir in the olive oil and some of the lemon juice. Season with salt and pepper and leave aside to absorb the dressing while you chop the parsley, mint and spring onions. Just before serving, mix the herbs with the bulgur, taste and add more lemon juice if necessary. It should taste fresh and lively.

To serve: arrange on a serving plate surrounded by lettuce leaves and little mounds of well seasoned tomato and cucumber dice. Garnish with rocket or sprigs of flat-leaf parsley. A few black olives wouldn't go amiss either if you enjoy them. Warm pitta or Middle Eastern flatbread is the perfect accompaniment.

Nutritional value per serving:

Calories: 196

Fats: 12g

Carbohydrates: 19g

Salt: 0.37g

Saturated fat: 1.7g

Fibre: 1.6g

spiced bulgur wheat pilaf

4 tablespoons olive oil

1 onion, chopped

450g (1lb) bulgur wheat (cracked wheat)

1 teaspoon ground cumin

1 teaspoon ground coriander seeds

1 teaspoon turmeric

1 teaspoon ground ginger

1 x 400g (14oz) tin of chopped tomatoes

salt and pepper

In a large heavy-based saucepan, heat the olive oil and gently sauté the onion in it for 10 minutes, or until softened.

Add the bulgur wheat and continue to cook for a further 2 minutes, stirring frequently. Add the spices and cook for 2 minutes more, or until the spices lose their raw aroma. Add the tomatoes with their liquid and 350ml (12fl oz) of water. Bring to the boil. Season, turn down the heat and simmer for 15 minutes, uncovered. (You may need a little more water towards the end of the cooking.)

Remove from heat and set aside for 10 minutes, covered with a clean tea towel, before serving.

Nutritional value per serving:

Calories: 388

Fats: 9g

Carbohydrates: 68g

Salt: 0.32g

Saturated fat: 1.3g

Fibre: 1g

warm **couscous** salad with yellow pesto

1 yellow pepper, about 200g (7oz) in total

4 tablespoons olive oil

10g ($^1/_2$oz) freshly grated Parmesan

300ml ($^1/_2$ pint) chicken or vegetable stock

10g ($^1/_2$oz) unsalted butter

250g (9oz) couscous

2 tablespoons snipped fresh chives

TIP

You can make the couscous in advance, and either serve cold or reheat in the oven, or even better, in a microwave. Stir in the yellow pesto just before serving or the couscous will lose some of its texture.

Nutritional value per serving:

Calories: 224

Fats: 10g

Carbohydrates: 23g

Salt: 0.21g

Saturated fat: 2.8g

Fibre: 0.6g

Grill the peppers as shown below. Transfer to a bowl with tongs and cover with cling film, leave to cool, then peel and discard the skins. Roughly chop the pepper flesh and place in a food processor or liquidiser and blend to a purée. Add the Parmesan and the remaining olive oil and blend again until smooth. Season to taste.

Place the stock in a pan and add the butter, then season to taste and bring to a simmer. Place the couscous in a large heatproof bowl and then pour over the stock mixture. Cover with cling film or foil and set aside for 5 minutes, then using a fork fluff up the grains so that they separate. Stir in the yellow pepper pesto and spoon into wide-rimmed bowls. Scatter over the chives and serve warm or cold.

How to grill peppers

Cut the pepper in half and remove the seeds, stalk and inner membrane. Place the pepper, cut side down in the tin and drizzle 1 tablespoon oil on top. Place under a hot grill for about 10 minutes or until the skin is blackened and blistered.

mixed wholegrain salad

50g (2oz) whole wheatberries, soaked for 12
   hours and drained, cooked and cooled

50g (2oz) pot barley, cooked and cooled

50g (2oz) buckwheat groats

Dressing

2 teaspoons brown miso

2 teaspoons cider vinegar

2 teaspoons soy sauce

1 teaspoon extra-virgin olive oil

Place the cooked wheatberries and barley in a bowl. Dry-roast the buckwheat in a pan over a medium heat, until it gives off a nutty aroma. Add plenty of water to cover, bring to the boil and simmer for 10-15 minutes until tender. Drain well and add to the other grains.

Mix together the ingredients for the dressing and stir into the grains. Serve at room temperature.

Nutritional value per serving:

Calories: 290

Fats: 3g

Carbohydrates: 62g

Salt: 1.38g

Saturated fat: 0.4g

Fibre: 1.9g

gujerati-style spinach with lemon & black pepper

2 tablespoons vegetable oil

1 garlic clove, crushed

1 teaspoon cumin seeds

1kg (2$^{1}/_{4}$lb) fresh spinach, well washed

juice and zest of 1 lemon

$^{1}/_{2}$ teaspoon sugar

4 tablespoons plain yogurt

$^{1}/_{4}$ teaspoon black peppercorns, coarsely
   crushed

salt

Heat the vegetable oil in a deep-sided frying pan, add the garlic and cumin seeds and fry for 1 minute to release their fragrance. Add the spinach, raise the heat and turn the spinach in the oil with the garlic and cumin. Add the lemon juice and zest and cook until the spinach has wilted. Stir in the sugar, yogurt and black pepper and adjust the seasoning. Serve hot.

TIP

This dish is rich in iron, calcium, folic acid and fibre, as well as Vitamins A, C and E.

Nutritional value per serving:

Calories: 129

Fats: 8g

Carbohydrates: 6g

Salt: 1.17g

Saturated fat: 1.1g

Fibre: 5.3g

wok-fried shiitake mushrooms

450g (1lb) shiitake mushrooms

1 tablespoon sesame oil

25g (1oz) fresh root ginger, peeled and finely
   chopped

1 large red chilli, deseeded and diced

75ml (3fl oz) soy sauce

10g ($^1/_2$oz) chopped fresh lemon balm

Wipe the mushrooms with dampened kitchen roll if necessary, then trim the stalks and slice.

Heat a wok until searing hot. Add the sesame oil and just as it begins to smoke, tip in the shiitake mushrooms and sauté gently for 1 minute. Add the ginger with chilli and soy sauce and stir-fry for a couple of minutes until the mushrooms are tender. Scatter over the lemon balm and spoon into a warmed side dish. Serve at once.

Nutritional value per serving:

Calories: 46

Fats: 3g

Carbohydrates: 2g

Salt: 3.61g

Saturated fat: 0.4g

Fibre: 0.1g

braised baby leeks with tapenade

75g (3oz) black olives, stoned (good quality)

2 large garlic cloves, finely chopped

10g ($\frac{1}{2}$oz) canned anchovy fillets, finely
   chopped

10g ($\frac{1}{2}$oz) sun-dried tomatoes, chopped
   (preserved in brine)

3 tablespoons olive oil

450g (1lb) baby leeks, trimmed

Place the olives in a food processor or liquidiser with the garlic, anchovies, sun-dried tomatoes and the olive oil, then blend to a smooth paste. Season to taste and add a little more oil if you think the tapenade is too thick – it should be the consistency of thick double cream.

Place the leeks in a pan of boiling salted water and cook for 2-4 minutes or until lightly cooked and just tender – the exact cooking time will depend on their size. Drain and quickly refresh in a bowl of ice-cold water, then pat dry with kitchen roll and arrange in a warmed serving dish. Drizzle over the tapenade and serve at once.

Nutritional value per serving:

Calories: 131

Fats: 11g

Carbohydrates: 4g

Salt: 1.51g

Saturated fat: 1.5g

Fibre: 3.1g

carrot, parsnip & cabbage with mustard seed

3 tablespoons sunflower oil

1 tablespoon black mustard seeds

1 chilli, deseeded and chopped

225g (8oz) carrots, coarsely grated

225g (8oz) parsnips, coarsely grated

225g (8oz) cabbage, finely shredded against
   the grain (see below)

2 tablespoons parsley, chopped

2 tablespoons mint, freshly chopped

salt, freshly ground pepper and sugar

freshly squeezed lemon juice, to taste

Heat the oil in a sauté pan and add the mustard seeds. They will start to pop almost instantly. Add the chopped chilli and stir and cook for a minute or so. Add the carrots, parsnips and cabbage. Toss over a medium heat for 2-3 minutes, then add the parsley and mint and toss again. Season with salt, freshly ground pepper and a little sugar. Add the lemon juice, taste and correct seasoning. Serve immediately.

How to shred red or white cabbage

Cut the cabbage into quarters and remove the hard centre. Turn each slice onto its side and slice thinly lengthways.

Nutritional value per serving:

Calories: 112

Fats: 7g

Carbohydrates: 10g

Salt: 0.21g

Saturated fat: 0.7g

Fibre: 3.9g

okra with tomatoes

700g (1½lb) fresh okra pods (ladies' fingers)
2 tablespoons oil
1 onion, chopped
2 garlic cloves, chopped
3 large tomatoes, chopped
1 chilli pepper, deseeded and chopped
1 teaspoon sugar
salt

Prepare the okra by trimming the stalks close to the pod. If you don't enjoy their glueyness – though lots of people do – don't hull, just trim off the stems, toss the pods with salt and a little vinegar and leave in a colander for an hour or two, by which time they will have yielded up their gloop; rinse well before using. Chunk.

Warm the oil in a heavy pan or casserole and gently fry the onion and garlic until soft – don't let it brown. Add the tomato, chilli and sugar and bubble up, squashing with a wooden spoon to encourage a rich little sauce. Stir in the okra, add a glass of water, and bubble up. Turn down the heat, put the lid on loosely and simmer for 30 minutes, until the pods are perfectly tender and the sauce deliciously rich and sticky. Or bake in the oven at 160°C/300°F/gas mark 2. Serve at room temperature, with quartered limes and chilli-pepper sauce on the side.

TIP

For a more substantial dish, include slivers of beef or pork tossed in the hot oil when you fry the onion and garlic, or finish with a handful of fresh prawns or shrimp.

This dish is a good source of calcium, folic acid and fibre, as well as Vitamins A and C.

Nutritional value per serving:
Calories: 124
Fats: 7g
Carbohydrates: 11g
Salt: 0.3g
Saturated fat: 0.7g
Fibre: 6.6g

delicious
desserts

SERVES 4

PREPARATION TIME: 5 MINUTES

COOKING TIME: 10 MINUTES

strawberries with bitter orange & honey

450g (1lb) big strawberries

4 tablespoons dark forest honey

2 bitter oranges, strips of zest and juice

Hull the strawberries and wipe them, but don't wash. Heat the honey in a small pan with the orange juice and zest and simmer for about 10 minutes, until the honey thickens and acquires the flavour of the orange. Dress the strawberries with the honey.

TIP

Lemon juice or sherry vinegar can replace the bitter orange juice.

Nutritional value per serving:

Calories: 83

Fats: 0g

Carbohydrates: 21g

Salt: 0.02g

Saturated fat: 0g

Fibre: 1.3g

four **melon** & ginger salad

25g (1oz) root ginger

100g (3$\frac{1}{2}$oz) demerara sugar

300ml (10fl oz) water

4 small melons e.g. Ogen, watermelon,
    cantaloupe, honeydew

large tub Greek yogurt

Grate the ginger into a small pan. Use a pastry brush dipped in a little of the water to brush down the grater and release all the bits. Add the sugar and water to the pan and cook slowly to dissolve the sugar. Bring to the boil and simmer fairly fast, keeping a watchful eye on the mixture for 10–15 minutes until it has reduced by half and become thick and syrupy. Pass through a fine sieve and chill.

Cut the melons into sections and remove the skin and seeds. Cut into smaller wedges or slices and arrange a few of each variety on dessert plates or one large platter. Spoon over the ginger syrup and serve with yogurt.

Nutritional value per serving:

Calories: 200

Fats: 6g

Carbohydrates: 32g

Salt: 0.24g

Saturated fat: 3.6g

Fibre: 1.5g

fruit kebabs

8 peaches or nectarines

8 apricots

24 cherries

16 strawberries

4 bananas

fresh lemon juice

orange liqueur (Cointreau or Grand Marnier)

175-225g (6-8oz) caster sugar

whipping cream

Cut the peaches or nectarines and apricots in halves, discarding the stones, and keep the strawberries and cherries whole. Peel the bananas and cut into large chunks about 2cm ($^3/_4$in) long and sprinkle with a little lemon juice. Mix the fruit in a bowl, sprinkle with orange liqueur, and macerate for about 15 minutes.

Thread the fruit onto skewers. Roll in caster sugar and barbecue for 5-8 minutes or until they start to caramelise. Serve immediately with a little softly whipped cream. For real excitement, pour some of the liqueur over each, set it alight and serve immediately. Otherwise just drink the marinade with the kebabs later on!

Nutritional value per kebab:

Calories: 109

Fats: 0g

Carbohydrates: 26g

Salt: 0.01g

Saturated fat: 0g

Fibre: 1.9g

plums baked in red wine & cranberry juice

50g (2oz) unsalted butter

8 plump red plums, halved and stoned

450ml (16fl oz) mixed red wine and cranberry
  juice

4 large sprigs mint, finely chopped

4 tablespoons brown caster sugar

Preheat the oven to 180°C/350°F/gas mark 4.

Rub the bottom of a shallow casserole pan with half the butter. Sprinkle with half the sugar and lay the plums on top, cut side down. Pour over the wine and cranberry juice, and sprinkle with the mint.

Dot the rest of the butter on top and dust with the remaining sugar.

Bake for 20 minutes.

Nutritional value per serving:

Calories: 252

Fats: 10g

Carbohydrates: 31g

Salt: 0.04g

Saturated fat: 6.5g

Fibre: 1.7g

scented pears

1 bottle full-bodied soft red wine

6 tablespoons lavender or other fragrant honey

2 tablespoons black peppercorns, tied in a
   muslin bag

6 sprigs lavender flowers

juice and zest of 1 lemon

6 ripe pears, peeled with the stem attached

6 sprigs of lavender flowers and mint to
   decorate

Combine the wine, honey, peppercorns, lavender flowers and lemon juice and zest in a large, heavy-bottomed pan. Bring to the boil and cook for 2 minutes.

Reduce the heat, add the pears and simmer, very gently, for 10 minutes. Remove from the heat and allow to cool. Serve the pears with a little of the cooking liquid and decorated with the lavender blossom and mint.

Nutritional value per serving:

Calories: 186

Fats: 0g

Carbohydrates: 27g

Salt: 0.04g

Saturated fat: 0g

Fibre: 3.3g

rhubarb filo parcels

700g (1½lb) rhubarb

110g (4oz) brown sugar

1 teaspoon chopped root ginger

50g (2oz) butter

6 sheets filo pastry

150ml (5fl oz) very low-fat fromage frais or
  Greek yogurt

Preheat the oven to 220°C/425°F/gas mark 7. Butter a large baking tray. Trim the rhubarb and cut into 2.5cm (1in) lengths. Place in a single layer in a large ovenproof dish. Sprinkle over the sugar and the ginger. Cover with a piece of foil and bake for 20 minutes or until the rhubarb is tender and has released its juices. Remove from the oven, cool and strain. Discard any excess juice.

Melt the butter in a small pan. Lay one sheet of filo pastry on the work surface and brush it with melted butter. Lay a second sheet on top and brush again. Cut into six 12.5cm (5in) squares. Place a heaped teaspoonful of the rhubarb in the centre of each square, followed by a teaspoonful of fromage frais. Make into purse shapes as shown below and place on the tray. Bake for 15 minutes until golden brown.

How to make filo parcels

Place the filling on the centre of each square of filo pastry. Take opposite corners and pinch together. Repeat with remaining two corners and twist together well.

Nutritional value per serving:

Calories: 278

Fats: 8g

Carbohydrates: 48g

Salt: 0.89g

Saturated fat: 4.6g

Fibre: 1.5g

index

acknowledgments

The publishers would like to thank the following authors for permission to use the recipes reproduced on the pages indicated: **Darina Allen:** 24, 26, 48, 54, 82, 96, 100, 126, 140, 154, 164; **Hugo Arnold:** 66, 90, 130, 138, 142; **Ed Baines:** 50; **Aliza Baron-Cohen, Adrian Mercuri and Louisa J Walters:** 14, 16, 34, 36, 38, 64, 120, 122, 124, 128, 146; **Vatcharin Bhumichitr:** 58, 70, 76, 88, 108, 134; **Maddelena Bonino:** 84; **Conrad Gallagher:** 40, 60, 68, 74, 78, 80, 94, 98, 106, 116, 144, 150, 152; **Paul Gayler:** 44, 110, 148; **Elisabeth Luard:** 72, 156, 160; **Alison Price:** 46; **Oded Schwartz:** 86, 104, 132, 136, 168; **Michael van Straten:** 18, 20, 22, 30, 32, 42, 52, 56, 92, 102, 114, 118, 166; **Mandy Wagstaff:** 162, 170.

The publishers would like to thank the following photographers for permission to use the images reproduced on the pages indicated: **Martin Brigdale:** 59, 62, 71, 77, 89, 109, 112, 135; **Julie Dixon:** 87, 105, 133, 137, 169; **Gus Filgate:** 28, 41, 45, 51, 61, 69, 75, 79, 81, 95, 99, 107, 111, 117, 145, 149, 151, 153; **Michelle Garrett:** 85; **Georgia Glynn-Smith:** 1, 9, 158; **Jeremy Hopley:** 47; **Francine Lawrence:** 73, 157, 161; **Ray Main:** 2, 5, 7, 12, 19, 21, 23, 25, 27, 31, 33, 43, 49, 53, 55, 56, 57, 60, 67, 76, 78, 82, 83, 91, 93, 97, 101, 103, 106, 115, 119, 127, 131, 139, 141, 143, 155, 165, 167; **Juliet Piddington:** 15, 17, 35, 37, 39, 65, 121, 123, 125, 129; **Jean-Luc Scotto:** 64, 68, 98, 110, 136, 138, 144, 154, 170; **Sara Taylor:** 163, 171.